Contents

Free gift:

Please note: the eBook edition of this guide containtains the complete original text. You deserve that too. Email proof of purchase to info@mrbruff.com and I will send you the eBook edition for free.

A word from our wonderful sponsors

The Owl Education Institute is an established and unique company. Based in West London we have been offering intensive tuition in the core subjects – English, Mathematics and Science - for over 25 years. The company shamelessly promotes academic, traditional teaching with an emphasis on examination success. We offer high level tutoring in small, focused group with each teacher head hunted and selected for his or her individual expertise and brilliance. An excellent centre with an exceptional reputation, we are now proud sponsors of Mr Bruff and look forward to working with him in the year ahead.

Dedication

I would like to start this book by thanking those who have helped and supported along the way:

Sam Perkins, who designed the front cover of this book.

Sunny Ratilal, who designed the original front cover which was adapted for this edition.

Part 1

Introduction

Mary Shelley was only 19 years old when she wrote her most famous novel 'Frankenstein' in 1816. Today, nearly 200 years later, the book continues to be read and studied across the world. So what is it about this tale that keeps generation after generation so intrigued? Well, to begin with, the text covers issues which are just as relevant and frightening today as they were in the early nineteenth century.

"You may deduce an apt moral from my tale": so says Victor Frankenstein to Robert Walton, and so says Mary Shelley to her reader. In this eBook I shall look for this moral. Along the way I shall analyse language, structure, form, character, theme, context, genre and much more; I hope you find it useful.

If you find this revision guide valuable then please visit my YouTube Channel at youtube.com/mrbruff where you will find hundreds of videos focusing on English and English Literature. My videos have been viewed over 2 million times across 198 nations – I'd love you to subscribe and join in.

Many other bestselling Mr Bruff titles are available both in electronic and print form on the MrBruff.com website and Amazon.

Andrew Bruff
April 2017

Part 2

Chapter Summary

Letter 1: Captain Robert Walton writes to his sister. He is on a mission to the North Pole.

Letter 2: Walton feels alone and isolated.

Letter 3: The journey begins - everything is going well.

Letter 4: The ship gets stuck in ice. The sailors see a mysterious creature, then meet Dr Victor Frankenstein who is near death with fatigue. Frankenstein says he will tell his story the next day.

Chapter 1: Victor tells the story of his childhood. He grew up in Geneva, where his parents adopted a 5 year old (Elizabeth). Victor talks a lot about fate.

Chapter 2: Victor explains that he was interested in Science from his early childhood, and describes his good friend Henry Clerval.

Chapter 3: Victor's mother dies after contracting Scarlett Fever from Elizabeth. Aged 17, Victor goes off to University at Ingoldstadt.

Chapter 4: Victor begins to study obsessively, ignoring his friends and family. He studies anatomy and decides that he wants to create life from bits of dead people (nothing odd about that).

Chapter 5: Victor brings his creature to life, but is disgusted at how evil it looks. He runs away and bumps into his friend Henry Clerval. Victor collapses from exhaustion and Clerval slowly nurses him back to health over a number of months. During this whole period the reader doesn't know where the creature is or what it is doing!

Chapter 6: Victor receives a letter from Elizabeth which introduces the character of Justine - a lovely servant girl who is staying with the family in Geneva. Henry and Victor travel in the countryside and absolutely love it!

Chapter 7: Victor learns that his brother William has been murdered. Victor sees the creature and guesses that the creature was the murderer. Meanwhile, Justine is framed for the murder.

Chapter 8: Justine is executed for the murder of William. Frankenstein feels terrible because he knows it was the creature who committed the crime, but he doesn't want to tell anyone because they will all think he is mad.

Chapter 9: Victor travels off into the countryside to make himself feel a bit better.

Chapter 10: Victor meets the creature at the top of a mountain. The creature wants to tell Victor his story.

Chapter 11: The creature explains that his first experiences are of people being mean to him because of how he looks. He then hid out near the home of an old blind man and two others, Felix and Agatha.

Chapter 12: The creature secretly helps the family by cutting wood for them. This shows he is good.

Chapter 13: A woman called Safie arrives. She is somehow linked to Felix but she speaks a different language. Felix teaches her English and the creature listens along and learns the language too.

Chapter 14: The creature now hears Safie's story. She fell in love with Felix and disobeyed her father's orders to stop the relationship. She ran away to find him.

Chapter 15: The creature reads 'Paradise Lost'. He finds Victor's journal and learns the story of his creation. The creature decides to befriend De Lacey (the blind old man). De Lacey is kind, but then Felix comes home and attacks the creature.

Chapter 16: Rejected by everyone, the creature becomes obsessed with gaining revenge on his creator. He travels to Geneva and kills William, planting evidence on Justine so that she will be blamed for the crime. The creature tells Victor that he wants him to create a woman for him.

Chapter 17: Victor refuses, but the creature promises to disappear forever if Victor will do as he asks. In the end Victor agrees to create the creature's wife.

Chapter 18: Victor travels to England to research how to create the creature's girlfriend. Henry Clerval comes with him.

Chapter 19: Victor leaves Henry in Scotland whilst he rents a building in the Orkneys and begins building the creature's wife.

Chapter 20: Victor suddenly changes his mind and destroys his half completed creation. The creature is angry. Victor rows a boat into the ocean to dispose of the parts. When he comes ashore he is accused of murder.

Chapter 21: The murder victim is Henry Clerval. Frankenstein is locked up but eventually freed on a technicality. His father comes to take him home. Victor knows that the creature murdered Clerval.

Chapter 22: Victor returns home and marries Elizabeth.

Chapter 23: The creature kills Elizabeth. Victor's dad drops dead from shock. Victor begins hunting down the creature.

Chapter 24: This brings us back to Walton's ship. Victor has followed the creature all the way to the North Pole. Victor dies and the creature comes aboard. The creature says he now has no reason to live and will kill himself. Then the creature leaves.

Part 3

The Author - Mary Shelley

Much has been written about Mary Shelley and her flamboyant lifestyle. However, as with all literary study, it is only important to learn the details about the author's life which are reflected in the novel itself.

It often isn't relevant to study the writer's parents, but with Shelley it certainly is. Shelley's mother, Mary Wollstonecraft, was a famous feminist writer perhaps best known for 'A Vindication of the Rights of Woman' (1792).

In this text Wollstonecraft argues that women are not naturally inferior to men, but have become so through the lack of education available to them. This theme of feminism is one that Mary Shelley explores in 'Frankenstein', and a chapter on this topic can be found later in this guide.

Wollstonecraft died a few days after giving birth to Mary, following a birth related infection. There is no doubt that Mary would have felt a sense of guilt over her mother's death, and this is reflected in the novel through the character of Elizabeth. In the novel, Frankenstein's mother dies after catching Scarlet Fever from Elizabeth. Although the cause of death is different, the idea that a daughter can unwittingly be the cause of her mother's death holds a strong parallel with the writer's own life.

Sadly, death was a regular event in Shelley's experience and in 1815 one of her children died. The death of a child is clearly profound, and when 'Frankenstein' was written the next year it is no surprise to see death, and the desire to prevent it, forming such a major theme in the text. It is possible to read the novel as a text that deals with the guilt of a failed parent – Dr Frankenstein fails to care for and nurture the life he created, just as Shelley perhaps felt about her own child.

In 1814, Mary Shelley took a trip to Germany and stayed very close to Castle Frankenstein. In the 1600s this castle was the home of an alchemist who undertook experiments very similar to those completed by Dr Frankenstein in the novel. Could this have been part of the influence on the novel? Surely the use of the name 'Frankenstein' comes from this source.

The events surrounding the writing of the novel are well-known, but here is a summary. In 1816, Shelley went on holiday to Lake Geneva with a number of famous writers. The weather was poor, and to pass the time the holidaymakers told ghost stories. Byron, the holiday host, then challenged each guest to write a ghost story of their own and it is here that Shelley wrote 'Frankenstein'. At just 18 years of age, Shelley wrote what continues to be one of the most famous works of English Literature.

Part 4

The Context

'Frankenstein' was written in the early 1800s, at a time of great social and historical change. In the 1760s, Jean Jacques Rousseau's 'Emile' explored the nature of education and human beings. In this text, the writer argues that humans are born harmless, and that it is society which makes people either good or bad. Today we might call this the 'nature vs. nurture' debate, and it is certainly one of the major themes in 'Frankenstein'. Turn to page 35 of this guide for a detailed chapter.

The novel 'Frankenstein' is a horror text, and to make something truly horrific it needs to tap into the fears of its readers; Shelley did this brilliantly. In order to create a truly terrifying book, Mary Shelley based the foundations of her tale on a recent scientific development which had been frightening the public: Galvanism.

Luigi Galvani was a scientist who experimented on dead animals with electricity. He found that the limbs of animals could be caused to spasm if touched with an electric current. Giovanni Aldini, Galvani's nephew, took these experiments one step further and tried them out on the body of a human being. In 1803 a man named George Foster murdered his wife and child and was hanged for the crime. Shortly after the hanging, Aldini took the body and experimented on it with electricity! The results were detailed as follows:

'On the first application of the process to the face, the jaws of the deceased criminal began to quiver, and the adjoining muscles were horribly contorted, and one eye was actually opened. In the subsequent part of the process the right hand was raised and clenched, and the legs and thighs were set in motion'.

As you can see, this bears quite the similarity with the novel 'Frankenstein' where, in Chapter 5, we read:

'By the glimmer of the half-extinguished light, I saw the dull yellow eye of the creature open; it breathed hard, and a convulsive motion agitated its limbs.'

The similarities are uncanny – even down to the opening of just one eye! Mary Shelley based the ideas in her novel on real-life events: the experimentation of electricity with dead bodies. This made the novel extremely terrifying as readers would worry that what happened in the novel (the creature goes on an unstoppable murderous rampage) would happen in real life too. It could be argued that this is why the novel is still so popular. Today we experiment with cloning, stem cell research and artificial intelligence. Behind it all is the fear that the results of our creation will overpower us and cause chaos and devastation.

Part 5

Genre: Horror, Gothic or Science Fiction?

The genre into which 'Frankenstein' fits has been the cause of much debate. Perhaps the most obvious suggestion would be to class it as a work of horror - a book which aims to frighten its readers. Horror itself can be broken into two genres: supernatural and non-supernatural. Clearly this is a book that would fit into the 'non-supernatural' category, as it aims to scare readers through a plot rooted closely in reality. Horror literature is often based on the prevalent fears in society at the time of writing, just as we see in 'Frankenstein' (see the previous chapter on 'context' for more on this).

However, the novel can also be classed as a work of gothic fiction. Gothic fiction is closely linked to horror, but also adds elements of romanticism and fiction. Essentially, this means that romance and superstition are combined. Do we see this in 'Frankenstein'? The answer is yes. There are a number of romances that are interwoven into the tale, most notably that of Elizabeth and Victor. Gothic fiction also needs an element of realism, where many events are realistic and believable. Once again, we find this in Shelley's novel.

The third and final genre into which the book can be placed is science fiction. Science fiction novels tend to be futuristic tales where writers imagine how the scientific developments and understanding of the present time will affect the future. Although 'Frankenstein' is not set in the future, there is clearly the sense that it is based on a realistic progression of current scientific development.

There are many scientific comments throughout the novel. Perhaps the most obvious is seen where Frankenstein talks of "a theory which he had formed on the subject of electricity and galvanism". As you have already read in my chapter on 'context', galvanism was a real life discovery, and one on which much of the novel is based. By taking a real life scientific discovery and 'fast- forwarding' to the possible future outcome of this work, Shelley can be classed as a science fiction writer.

The novel offers much comment on the topic of science itself. Frankenstein begins Chapter 3 by praising the work of science, claiming that "the labours of men of genius, however erroneously directed, scarcely ever fail in ultimately turning to the solid advantage of mankind." At this point in the novel it seems that science is always to be praised, even if it is misguided. However, this opinion is changed by the end of the tale. In Chapter 24, Frankenstein's words of warning are very different as he cautions "avoid ambition, even it if be only the apparently innocent one of distinguishing yourself in science and discoveries". So why the dramatic change? Clearly Frankenstein thought that his creation would remain under his control, but this was not the case. The creature himself points out to his creator "thou hast made me more powerful than thyself; my height is superior to thine, my joints more supple". This quote is reminiscent of almost every sci-fi film I've ever seen. A more modern approach is the common theme that artificial intelligence or robots will overpower humans and take over the world. At the start of the novel Dr Frankenstein told us: "you may deduce an apt moral from my tale".

Surely this is it: "avoid ambition, even it if be only the apparently innocent one of distinguishing yourself in science and discoveries".

Part 6

Importance of the Title

Firstly, let's get one thing straight: Frankenstein is the name of the doctor, not the name of the creature. If you already knew that then you are in the top 1% of the country, because most people think Frankenstein is the name of the creature. So, the title shows us that this tale is primarily about the Doctor, Victor Frankenstein. This is backed up by the subtitle, which is sometime included and sometimes not.

The subtitle of this novel is 'The Modern Prometheus'. Prometheus is a character from Greek mythology who created mankind from clay. Obviously there is a parallel with 'Frankenstein' in the notion of someone creating life from inanimate source material, but there's more than that. In the original myth, Prometheus got in trouble for giving humans the gift of fire, which allowed human civilisation to develop. He was then bound to daily punishment. This is where the story gets a bit weird: Prometheus's punishment was to have his liver eaten by an eagle, before it grew back and happened again every day. OK, I know what you're thinking: 'that bit's not like 'Frankenstein''. But maybe it is.

In ancient Greece, the liver was thought to be connected to emotions, so the metaphorical punishment here is the daily torture of the emotions. In this reading, Victor's punishment is similar: he is subjected to repeated emotional torment as, one by one, his friends, family and loved ones are brutally murdered. The murders don't all happen at the same time - they are drawn out so that the punishment is more painful, hence the repeated eating of the livers.

Part 7

Setting

If the aim of Shelley's novel is to scare the reader, the setting is often used to help achieve this aim. This is no more apparent than when Frankenstein brings the creature to life in Chapter 5. Consider the following passage:

"It was on <u>a dreary night of November</u> that I beheld the accomplishment of my toils. With an anxiety that almost amounted to agony, I collected the instruments of life around me, that I might infuse a spark of being into the lifeless thing that lay at my feet. It was already <u>one in the morning; the rain pattered dismally against the panes</u>, and my candle was nearly burnt out, when, by the glimmer of the half-extinguished light, I saw the dull yellow eye of the creature open; it breathed hard, and a convulsive motion agitated its limbs.

How can I describe my emotions at this catastrophe, or how delineate the wretch whom with such infinite pains and care I had endeavoured to form? His limbs were in proportion, and I had selected his features as beautiful. Beautiful! Great God! His yellow skin scarcely covered the work of muscles and arteries beneath; his hair was of a lustrous black, and flowing; his teeth of a pearly whiteness; but these luxuriances only formed a more horrid contrast with his watery eyes, that seemed almost of the same colour as the dun-white sockets in which they were set, his shrivelled complexion and straight black lips".

Now let's take some time to analyse those phrases related to setting, underlined:

To begin, the events take place on 'a dreary night of November' at 'one in the morning'. Shelley is using two tried and tested horror conventions here:

1. The story takes place in November. Why? Because November is a time of dark evenings and bleak, relentless weather. If this scene took place on a sunny August afternoon would it have the same effect? Clearly not! No, winter time is a classic horror story setting. In fact, we see a lot of the events take place during this period of the year. In Chapter 2, Robert Walton's own story begins in a "winter" that "has been dreadfully severe". Shelley sets the scary scenes in the most frightening season of winter.

2. Why does the scene take place at 'one in the morning'? This late night setting conjures up images in the reader's head of isolation and danger. Everyone who could possibly help Frankenstein is tucked up in bed, and that isolation creates fear. Night time is also associated with fear because at night we cannot see so clearly what is around us and our minds play tricks on us as we imagine things that aren't really there. With our sense of sight diminished our other senses increase and so we hear strange noises that we might not have before heard. Has that ever happened to you in bed at night? It can seem like someone is walking on the landing outside your room, but it's simply the creaking noises of the house which otherwise go undetected. Once again our mind plays tricks on

us as we become sure that something threatening is near us. Shelley knew all this, and masterfully uses setting to create a foreboding atmosphere.

The weather is also used to convey meaning; Shelley uses the literary device of pathetic fallacy, giving human characteristics to the weather. Because of this, the reader is on edge when reading that "the rain pattered dismally against the panes". The bad weather foreshadows the ensuing bad events. In fact, the word 'dismally' comes from the Latin dies mali which means 'evil days'. By describing even the weather as 'evil' it creates tension in the reader who is sure that something bad is about to happen (and they're not wrong).

It is not just in Chapter 5 that Shelley uses the setting of night to create fear. I wondered whether Victor was actually a vampire, given the amount of the story which takes place at night (that's a bad joke – don't write that in an exam). In Chapter 7, Frankenstein explains that "it was completely dark when I arrived in the environs of Geneva". Yes, Shelley is very keen on setting the scary moments in the dead of night to create fear. Victor puts it best himself when he explains in Chapter 23 "I had been calm during the day, but so soon as night obscured the shapes of objects, a thousand fears arose in my mind". Just like the reader, Victor gets scared at night time; I bet he sleeps with the landing light on.

The final way in which Shelley uses setting to create fear is in the geographical setting of the story. Knowing that the initial primary readership of her novel would be from England, the story begins with Robert Walton's words which reassure the reader that he is 'already far north of London'. Now let's map out the different settings and how far away they are from England:

- Robert Walton is soon stuck in ice around the North Pole, 2,600 miles away from England.
- The story then turns to Victor, who himself was born in Naples, 1,200 miles from England.
- Victor goes to University at Ingolstadt, 660 miles from England.

As you can see, a horrific tale which began thousands of miles away is beginning to get closer and closer to the home of English readers. As the tale progresses, Victor comes to the UK to conduct research needed for the creation of his female monster. It is with trepidation that the reader recognises the places of his travels: "Arthur's Seat, St. Bernard's Well, and the Pentland Hills". Finally, in Chapter 20, we read these terrifying words: "I have dwelt many months in the heart of England". The events of the tale, which at first seemed so distant, have become closer and closer to the English readership. This would scare the reader as they would irrationally fear that the monster could be right around the corner from them as they read! The familiarity of the setting is too close for comfort and the reader could not help but be panicked.

Part 8

Character Analysis of Dr Frankenstein

One of the most interesting aspects of the novel is the gradual breakdown of Victor Frankenstein. When he began his scientific work it was with the motives and passion that we might expect to see in all scientists. Frankenstein admits that he was "smitten with the thirst for knowledge". His motives are revealed to be somewhat egocentric when he explains "what glory would attend the discovery if I could banish disease from the human frame and render man invulnerable to any but a violent death!" The key word here is 'glory'; Victor Frankenstein begins as a young and ambitious scientist whose thirst for knowledge is fed by a desire for critical acclaim. Although this may be a tad selfish, we cannot criticise this viewpoint too heavily – Victor is simply an intelligent and ambitious young man. However, this soon begins to change.

In Chapter 4 the reader begins to feel worried by Victor's admission that "two years passed in this manner, during which I paid no visit to Geneva, but was engaged, heart and soul, in the pursuit of some discoveries which I hoped to make". This is the first sign that Frankenstein is becoming obsessed with his work and is neglecting other crucial areas of life.

By the end of Chapter 4 things have grown even worse, as Frankenstein's' "cheek had grown pale with study, and my person had become emaciated with confinement". Not only is he physically drained but his mental stage begins to show signs of trouble as he explains that his work took "an irresistible hold of my imagination". At this point the reader can sense that something wicked is going to happen. Mary Shelley is here using foreshadowing, a literary device where the writer leaves clues about future events. The foreshadowing here is clear: this doctor, who is experimenting with very serious areas of study, is becoming irrational and obsessed. This creates fear in the reader because they imagine that something is going to go wrong.

At the end of Chapter 4, only pages before the creature comes to life, Frankenstein has sunk even lower:

"Every night I was oppressed by a slow fever, and I became nervous to a most painful degree; the fall of a leaf startled me, and I shunned my fellow creatures as if I had been guilty of a crime".

By this point in the novel we now behold a character who is exhausted, obsessed, unwell, paranoid and isolated: not the kind of guy you'd want as your doctor!

In Chapter 5, the creature comes to life. This is the climax of the novel and therefore the mental state of the man in charge is crucial. Nevertheless, we hear these worrying words from Victor: "for this I had deprived myself of rest and health". By his own admission, Frankenstein has deprived himself of everything he needs. The result? He cannot cope with what he creates:

"Unable to endure the aspect of the being I had created, I rushed out of the room and continued a long time traversing my bed-chamber, unable to compose my mind to sleep. At length lassitude succeeded to the tumult I had before endured, and I threw myself on the bed in my clothes, endeavouring to seek a few moments of forgetfulness. But it was in vain; I slept".

Shelley is here using her writer's craft to full effect. After four chapters of waiting, the creature has finally been brought to life. However, Shelley then changes topic and writes about how Frankenstein is feeling. All throughout this section of the novel, where Clerval comes and nurses his friend, the reader is desperate to hear about the creature. What is it doing? Where is it? Of course, what Shelley is doing is leaving it to the reader's imagination. By leaving topics unexplained they become more frightening. This is because the reader has to imagine in their own mind just what is taking place. Each reader will imagine something different depending on what is the scariest to them: for some it will be the idea that the creature is off in the streets; others will be terrified that the creature is lurking behind the door about to jump out at any second. This convention of horror writing is used very successfully in this passage.

By the end of the novel, Frankenstein seems to have undergone a change of character. He moves from being a man of science to a man of the supernatural. In Chapter 24 he expounds "Elizabeth and my departed friends, who even now prepare for the reward of my tedious toil and horrible pilgrimage". The meaning of this quote is clear: Elizabeth, Clerval and Justine are in heaven getting the party ready for me. This is one of the first mentions of religion that Victor makes – could it be that he has believed in God all along, or has the horror of what he has been through forced him to re-evaluate his belief system?

The final piece of the puzzle is found later in the same chapter, where Victor mentions a moment "after a slight repose, during which the spirits of the dead hovered round and instigated me to toil and revenge". Now it seems that the spirits of his dead friends are floating around him and telling him to go and kill the monster. Up until this point the events of the novel have been based loosely on scientific developments, but now we see a completely supernatural moment. This shows that the rational, educated and passionate scientist has totally changed. Whether he has become an hallucinating mad-man or has simply now turned to a belief in the supernatural is up to you to decide!

Part 9

Character Analysis of the Creature

Long before we meet the creature, we hear Frankenstein's evil description of him. In the beginning of Chapter 5 alone, Frankenstein refers to his creation as a 'catastrophe', a 'wretch' and 'horrid'. This is quickly followed with religious language related to the devil, such as 'demoniacal corpse' and 'filthy daemon'. All of this imagery paints a picture in the reader's mind of a savage beast. However, this soon changes when we get to meet the creature himself.

In Chapter 11 we hear, albeit through Frankenstein's retelling, the voice of the creature. It is with some surprise that we learn the creature is an intelligent and articulate being. One of the most obvious examples of this comes when it describes the setting as "divine a retreat as Pandemonium appeared to the demons of hell". This is an intertextual reference to 'Paradise Lost', John Miltion's epic poem of over 1,000 lines from the 17th Century. The poem tells the story of the fall of man, focusing on Adam and Eve and their fall into sin.

The creature's reference is specifically linked to Adam and Eve's discovery of the fallen world upon leaving Eden. This reference can be seen as symbolic, as the creature himself found the world to be a corrupt and fallen place. So, as well as showing the creature to be intelligent, the quote is also one of many Biblical references in the creature's life.

The life of the creature holds many similarities with the creation story from the book of Genesis in the Bible. In Genesis chapter 1, the first thing God says is 'there be light: and there was light'. In the same way, the creature's first experience is light, seen when he explains: "a stronger light pressed upon my nerves". In the Bible, Adam and Eve live in the Garden of Eden, where all plants and animals are given to them for their pleasure. This is very similar to the creature's experience in "the forest near Ingolstadt...sometimes I tried to imitate the pleasant songs of the birds...I distinguished the insect from the herb, and by degrees, one herb from another". These similarities with the Bible creation story are used by Shelley to symbolise how Frankenstein took on a god- like role in creating life (more on that in another chapter).

Whereas the Biblical references are subtle in the first half of the text, they become less so in Chapter 15. When talking again about 'Paradise Lost', the creature explains that he was:

"moved every feeling of wonder and awe that the picture of an omnipotent God warring with his creatures was capable of exciting. I often referred the several situations, as their similarity struck me, to my own. Like Adam, I was apparently united by no link to any other being in existence; but his state was far different from mine in every other respect. He had come forth from the hands of God a perfect creature, happy and prosperous, guarded by the especial care of his Creator; he was allowed to converse

with and acquire knowledge from beings of a superior nature, but I was wretched, helpless, and alone".

This is a reference to Adam's desire for a partner. In the Bible, Adam was discontented on his own and so God made Eve, a woman, to be his companion. The creature wants the same. So what does it all mean? Mary Shelley seems to be criticising the God of the Bible in these passages. Perhaps she feels a sense of unfairness that God made his creation and then abandoned them in her view, just as Frankenstein abandoned the creature.

One of the most shocking discoveries the reader makes about the creature is that he is, in fact, good natured. Juxtaposed to the evil description given by Dr Frankenstein, we read in Chapter 12 that:

"kindness moved me sensibly. I had been accustomed, during the night, to steal a part of their store for my own consumption, but when I found that in doing this I inflicted pain on the cottagers, I abstained and satisfied myself with berries, nuts, and roots which I gathered from a neighbouring wood."

This presentation of the creature as intelligent plays a big part in the 'nature vs. nurture' debate which can be read about in Part 17 of this study guide.

Part 10

Similarities Between the Creature and Other Characters

Shelley presents a number of instances where the monster appears to be very similar to Frankenstein (or perhaps Frankenstein appears to be like his creation). Consider the following passage from Chapter 1, where Frankenstein talks about how his parents treated him:

"I was their plaything and their idol, and something better - their child, the innocent and helpless creature bestowed on them by heaven, whom to bring up to good, and whose future lot it was in their hands to direct to happiness or misery, according as they fulfilled their duties towards me".

Here we can see that, like the monster, Victor's destiny is in the hands of his parents; if they raise him well he will be happy, but if they raise him poorly he will be miserable. As I shall explore in the 'nature vs. nurture' chapter, there is a strong parallel with the monster's words in Chapter 10: "I was benevolent and good; misery made me a fiend. Make me happy, and I shall again be virtuous". So here is the first strong similarity: both Frankenstein and the monster believe that their creators (natural or artificial) have the power to shape their characters through the way they are treated.

The creature, when trying to help out Felix and Agatha in Chapter 12, speaks of his good motives, explaining that "I thought (foolish wretch!) that it might be in my power to restore happiness to these deserving people". This mirrors the motives of Frankenstein, who only undertook the experiments in the first place to "renew life where death had apparently devoted the body to corruption." Whilst each seemed to have good intentions, both the creature and the doctor knew in hindsight that their plans were ridiculous. The monster calls himself a "foolish wretch" for thinking he could do good for others, and Victor admits to Robert Walton that his intentions were "madness".

When wrongly suspected of Clerval's murder, Victor is treated with disdain by the Irish locals:

"As I was occupied in fixing the boat and arranging the sails, several people crowded towards the spot. They seemed much surprised at my appearance, but instead of offering me any assistance, whispered together with gestures that at any other time might have produced in me a slight sensation of alarm. As it was, I merely remarked that they spoke English, and I therefore addressed them in that language. "My good friends," said I, "will you be so kind as to tell me the name of this town and inform me where I am?"

Here we can see that Frankenstein is getting to experience a glimpse of the creature's daily life, being pre-judged as evil by everyone around him. However, it is not only Frankenstein who has similarities with the monster.

When interrogated for the murder which she did not commit, Justine explains:

"I did confess, but I confessed a lie. I confessed, that I might obtain absolution; but now that falsehood lies heavier at my heart than all my other sins. The God of heaven forgive me! Ever since I was condemned, my confessor has besieged me; he threatened and menaced, until I almost began to think that I was the monster that he said I was. He threatened excommunication and hell fire in my last moments if I continued obdurate. Dear lady, I had none to support me; all looked on me as a wretch doomed to ignominy and perdition. What could I do? In an evil hour I subscribed to a lie; and now only am I truly miserable."

A key quotation here is: "He threatened and menaced, until I almost began to think that I was the monster that he said I was". This quotation suggests that people are influenced by the way they are treated, but Shelley's use of the specific word 'monster' shows that she is making an important point: if we treat people as monsters, monsters they will become.

Finally, the creature can also be seen to have lines of similarity with Henry Clerval. In Chapter 18, we read that Clerval "was alive to every new scene, joyful when he saw the beauties of the setting sun, and more happy when he beheld it rise and recommence a new day". Does this not bear a striking resemblance to this comment from the monster in Chapter 12: "My spirits were elevated by the enchanting appearance of nature". It seems that both Clerval and the monster took much pleasure and delight in nature (more on that in a future chapter).

So what is Shelley's message? Well, perhaps she is saying that all of us are capable of becoming a monster – that the monster in the story is not so far removed from the 'good' characters. Or perhaps the point is that all those who are evil are also capable of good? This is a line of thought which I shall further explore in the chapter on 'nature vs. nurture'.

Part 11

Shelley's Use of Language

Although I have covered some of this topic in the chapter on setting, it is worth looking in more detail at a couple of specific examples where Shelley has used language for effect.

In Chapter 10, Frankenstein is trying to escape his depression and so journeys into the countryside. Have a read of this passage:

"I retired to rest at night; my slumbers, as it were, waited on and <u>ministered</u> to by the assemblance of grand shapes which I had contemplated during the day. They <u>congregated</u> round me; the unstained snowy mountain-top, the glittering pinnacle, the pine woods, and ragged bare ravine, the eagle, soaring amidst the clouds—they all gathered round me and bade me be at <u>peace</u>.

Where had they fled when the next morning I awoke? All of <u>soul</u>-inspiriting fled with sleep, and dark melancholy clouded every thought. The rain was pouring in torrents, and thick mists hid the summits of the mountains, so that I even saw not the faces of those mighty friends. Still I would penetrate their misty veil and seek them in their cloudy retreats. What were rain and storm to me? My mule was brought to the door, and I resolved to ascend to the summit of Montanvert. I remembered the effect that the view of the tremendous and ever-moving glacier had produced upon my mind when I first saw it. It had then filled me with a <u>sublime</u> ecstasy that gave <u>wings to the soul</u> and allowed it to soar".

As highlighted underlined, Shelley uses a vast array of religious imagery to show how Frankenstein is feeling at peace and serenity in this setting. However, the language then changes in the following paragraphs:

"The ascent is <u>precipitous</u>, but the path is <u>cut</u> into continual and short windings, which enable you to surmount the perpendicularity of the mountain. It is a scene terrifically <u>desolate</u>. In a thousand spots the traces of the winter avalanche may be perceived, where trees lie <u>broken</u> and <u>strewed</u> on the ground, some entirely <u>destroyed</u>, others <u>bent</u>, leaning upon the jutting rocks of the mountain or transversely upon other trees. The path, as you ascend higher, is intersected by ravines of snow, down which stones continually roll from above; one of them is particularly <u>dangerous</u>, as the slightest sound, such as even speaking in a loud voice, produces a <u>concussion</u> of air sufficient to draw destruction upon the head of the speaker.

Clearly the language has moved from religious to bleak, but why? Well, shortly after this moment, Frankenstein meets the creature in the mountains. Shelley is therefore using language to foreshadow that something bad is about to happen. The juxtaposition of positive with negative language heightens the impact of the negativity upon the reader.

This is a technique used often in the novel. Consider the following extract from Victor's Chapter 18 journey with Clerval:

"the waves dash with fury the base of the mountain, where the <u>priest</u> and his mistress were overwhelmed by an avalanche and where their dying voices are still said to be heard amid the pauses of the nightly wind; I have seen the mountains of La Valais, and the Pays de Vaud; but this country, Victor, pleases me more than all those wonders. The mountains of Switzerland are more <u>majestic</u> and strange, but there is a charm in the banks of this <u>divine</u> river that I never before saw equalled. Look at that castle which overhangs yon precipice; and that also on the island, almost concealed amongst the foliage of those lovely trees; and now that group of labourers coming from among their vines; and that village half hid in the recess of the mountain. Oh, surely the <u>spirit</u> that inhabits and guards this place has a <u>soul</u> more in harmony with man than those who pile the glacier or retire to the inaccessible peaks of the mountains of our own country." Clerval! Beloved friend! Even now it delights me to record your words and to dwell on the <u>praise</u> of which you are so eminently deserving".

Once again Shelley uses religious language to convey the peace the characters find in the natural landscape. However, it also relaxes the reader and sets them up into a false sense of security that everything is OK. Only three chapters later do we discover that Clerval is dead.

Part 12

Shelley's Use of Structure

The Greek philosopher Aristotle, around the year 335 BC, wrote 'Poetics', a book which included theories on narrative structure. He analysed Greek tragedy as a genre and defined some of the main characteristics which he felt were essential in works of tragedy. In the 19th Century, building on the work of Aristotle, the German novelist Gustav Freytag proposed that all plots can be divided into a five part structure:

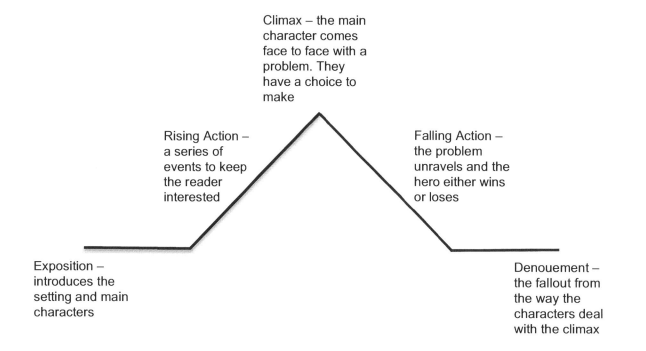

Climax – the main character comes face to face with a problem. They have a choice to make

Rising Action – a series of events to keep the reader interested

Falling Action – the problem unravels and the hero either wins or loses

Exposition – introduces the setting and main characters

Denouement – the fallout from the way the characters deal with the climax

If we apply this model to 'Frankenstein' we need to look at the story in chronological order, not the order in which it is told.

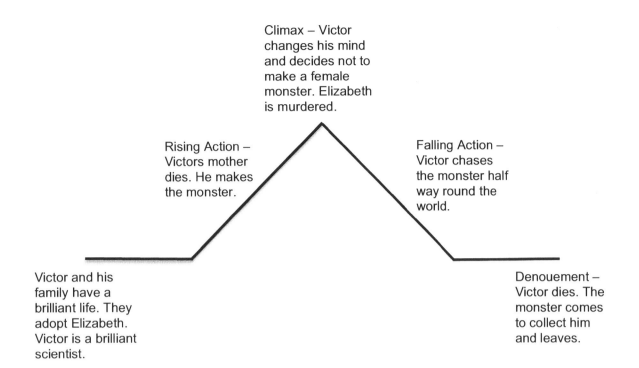

Climax – Victor changes his mind and decides not to make a female monster. Elizabeth is murdered.

Rising Action – Victors mother dies. He makes the monster.

Falling Action – Victor chases the monster half way round the world.

Victor and his family have a brilliant life. They adopt Elizabeth. Victor is a brilliant scientist.

Denouement – Victor dies. The monster comes to collect him and leaves.

As you can see, the novel fits neatly in with Freytag's model. However, the novel isn't told in chronological order. The novel actually begins near the denouement in Walton's ship. It is then followed by a series of flashbacks which, ultimately, lead back to the denouement on Walton's ship. This is what we call a cyclical narrative structure:

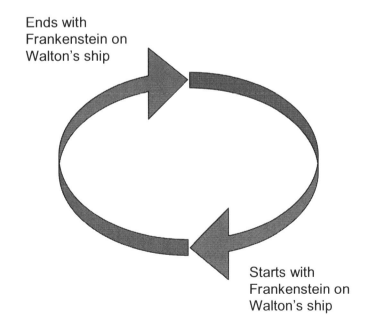

Ends with Frankenstein on Walton's ship

Starts with Frankenstein on Walton's ship

This cyclical structure is used by Shelley to convey one of the major themes of the novel: fate. Fate (explored fully in another chapter) is the idea that the events in our lives are pre-determined and set – we can't get away from them. In this way, the cyclical novel which ends up just where it started reflects how there is no escape from fate: if you run away from it you will only end up back where you started.

Shelley also uses structure within chapters to create tension. In Chapter 5, the creature is finally brought to life and the reader gets a glimpse of what it looks like. This is a hugely significant moment in the novel, but then the topic changes. We read that Victor "escaped and rushed downstairs". He ran into the streets, bumped into Clerval, fainted from fatigue and was nursed back to health over a number of months. In all this time the reader has one simple question: where is the creature? But this question remains unanswered for quite some time. Shelley is here using structure to create suspense, changing topic onto less interesting events and making the reader imagine what is happening with the creature. This is one way in which Shelley uses structure to create tension in the novel. It also makes the reader keen to read on as we want to know exactly what the creature is up to!

Part 13

The Role of Women

As already noted Shelley's mother, Mary Wollstonecraft, was a famous advocate of women's rights. I believe that Shelley followed in her mother's footsteps, and there is much evidence to support this in the novel. Some could argue that the heavily male dominated plot, along with the fact that so many women die in the novel, makes it hard to argue for a feminist interpretation; I disagree.

Firstly, let me give you a few brief notes on the treatment of women in 1800s England:

- When a woman married, she became the legal property of her husband
- Women could not testify in court
- Women could not vote
- It was believed that women were incapable of rational thought
- Many female writers published their works anonymously or under male pseudonyms in order to boost book sales (Mary Shelley published 'Frankenstein' anonymously). Although women could publish, women's literature was not taken as seriously as that written by men. In order to be taken seriously, many women published anonymously.

There are a number of key quotations worth exploring in the novel in relation to the treatment of women. To begin with, let's look at how Frankenstein's father treated his wife:

"He strove to shelter her, as a fair exotic is sheltered by the gardener, from every rougher wind and to surround her with all that could tend to excite pleasurable emotion in her soft and benevolent mind".

This quotation suggests that women are like pets – it certainly doesn't suggest equality. There is also the idea that women are objects of pleasure to their husbands.

Throughout the novel, women are described in terms of their physical beauty. Even Elizabeth, when writing to Victor, describes Justine as 'extremely pretty'. In the same letter she writes about 'the pretty Miss Mansfield' and 'her ugly sister'. Finally, there is mention of 'a lively pretty Frenchwoman'. In stark contrast to this, none of the male characters is ever referred to as handsome, but are defined more through their intellect, such as when Robert Walton describes Victor as possessing 'unparalleled eloquence'. Here Shelley is pointing out the objectification of women which sees them as little more than objects of physical desire and gratification.

Even when Justine is facing her impending death, Victor's description of her is sordidly sexual:

"The appearance of Justine was calm. She was dressed in mourning, and her countenance, always engaging, was rendered, by the solemnity of her feelings, exquisitely beautiful".

Did you see that? 'Beautiful'! A woman accused of murder and waiting for her sentence is described as 'beautiful'.

It is frustrating to see Elizabeth so accepting of the way she is treated. On hearing that she is betrothed to Victor, she tells him "You well know, Victor, that our union had been the favourite plan of your parents ever since our infancy. We were told this when young, and taught to look forward to it as an event that would certainly take place". Here we see that Elizabeth seems to have no choice or opinion on the matter of her arranged marriage. Victor's view of the marriage is not much better.

Victor's proposed marriage to Elizabeth is presented as a business transaction, organised without any emotion, female involvement or mention of love by Victor who casually explains that "it was understood that my union with Elizabeth should take place immediately on my return". This theory is further enforced when he later talks about how he "might claim Elizabeth". Once again, women are seen as objects destined to provide pleasure for men.

So did Mary Shelley agree with this treatment of women? Absolutely not! Society at the time proposed that women were incapable of rational thought, but this is clearly disproven in the novel. When the sexist treatment of women is fully established, Shelley begins to challenge it. This is seen clearly in Chapter 8 of the novel. At Justine's trial, the innocently accused speaks with such intellect and eloquence – Shelley has deliberately written a fantastic speech here:

"I commit my cause to the justice of my judges, yet I see no room for hope. I beg permission to have a few witnesses examined concerning my character, and if their testimony shall not overweigh my supposed guilt, I must be condemned, although I would pledge my salvation on my innocence".

Similarly, Elizabeth's defence of her friend is equally impressive:

"I am," said she, "the cousin of the unhappy child who was murdered, or rather his sister, for I was educated by and have lived with his parents ever since and even long before his birth. It may therefore be judged indecent in me to come forward on this occasion, but when I see a fellow creature".

Remember, this was written at a time when women could not testify in court! Both Justine and Elizabeth present such rational, systematic lines of argument that they clearly outdo the males in the book. In fact, these are two of the most intelligent passages in the complete novel. Shelley is here showing just how intelligent and articulate women can be.

Having shown us how women should not be treated, the next female character we are introduced to gives hints at a better approach. Shelley's next female focus is the character of Safie. Safie is a character who is encouraged to challenge the treatment of women by her mother:

"She instructed her daughter in the tenets of her religion and taught her to aspire to higher powers of intellect and an independence of spirit forbidden to the female followers of Muhammad".

Encouraged by her mother to think for herself, Safie demonstrates a high level of independence. This is seen when she disagreed with her father's plans and "resolved in her own mind the plan of conduct that it would become her to pursue in this emergency." Shelley uses the French character as a model of how English women should act and be treated.

Shelley further criticises the subject of male dominance when Victor thinks about the female creature he is planning on creating. Although the creature explains that the woman will do as he wants her to, Victor realises with shock that "she, who in all probability was to become a thinking and reasoning animal, might refuse to comply with a compact made before her creation". This line is one of the most significant when it comes to the role of women in society. Shelley is saying, through the observations of Victor, that women are individuals with their own minds, and the roles pre-determined for them by a patriarchal society, are unjust.

Part 14

Religious Imagery and Metaphor

Throughout the novel there are many striking similarities between Shelley's text and the Bible.

One of the most obvious links with the Bible is the concept that Dr Frankenstein 'plays God' and creates life. In the book of Genesis we read 'so God created man in his own image, in the image of God created he him' (Genesis 1:27). Just as God is the creator of mankind in the Bible, Dr Frankenstein is the creator of life in the novel, speaking in grandiose tones when he declares "a new species would bless me as its creator and source".

In the Bible, God created mankind for good – to enjoy the Earth and relationship with Him. However, mankind sinned and turned away from God, causing God to lament that 'the wickedness of man was great in the earth, and that every imagination of the thoughts of his heart was only evil continually'. (Genesis 6:5). This is very similar to Dr Frankenstein's disappointment with his creation. Victor laments "I considered the being whom I had cast among mankind, and endowed with the will and power to effect purposes of horror".

In the Bible, God is so disgusted with the actions of his creation that He decides 'I will destroy man whom I have created from the face of the earth' (Genesis 6:7). In the novel, Dr Frankenstein has similar thoughts, declaring "I ardently wished to extinguish that life which I had so thoughtlessly bestowed".

So, up to this point, the comparisons are clear: both God and Victor create life with good intentions but, disgusted in how their creations act, wish to undo what they have made. So what does it all mean? Well, Mary Shelley was an ardent atheist, so it is likely she is using her Biblical comparisons as a criticism of Christianity. The reader will probably feel that Dr Frankenstein is wrong in desiring to destroy his creation. In the same way, perhaps Shelley is suggesting that God was wrong to destroy his own creation (save for Noah and his family) in the book of Genesis. The Biblical criticism continues when the creature finally speaks to Dr Frankenstein.

In Chapter 10, the creature faces his maker and challenges him. Up until this point, the Biblical allusions have been fairly subtle, but Shelley uses the words of the creature to make her points more overt in this section of the novel. The creature challenges Victor by arguing "You accuse me of murder, and yet you would, with a satisfied conscience, destroy your own creature". It is possible to see this quote as a direct challenge from Shelley to the God of the Bible: "you murdered almost all of humanity because they were engaged in sins such as murder". Shelley is here using the words of the creature to criticise what she sees as hypocrisy in the Bible story. However, there are other Biblical allusions to explore too.

In Chapter 17, the creature speaks to Victor as if he is indeed God, pleading with him "If you grant my prayer...you shall never behold me again". The use of the religious word 'prayer' is very important here. To the creature, Dr Frankenstein IS God. However, the creature is made to feel not like a valued creation, but like the devil himself, stating 'like the archangel who aspired to omnipotence, I am chained in an eternal hell." This quote is a reference to Satan. Although the Bible does not refer to Satan as an Archangel, but simply an angel, the reference is clearly meant to refer to Satan. Dr Frankenstein's aspirations to become a god like creator have failed.

Part 15

True Happiness - Romanticism vs. Enlightenment

'Frankenstein' contains two contrasting ideas about the source of happiness in life. To begin with, Victor Frankenstein admits to Robert Walton that he was "smitten with the thirst for knowledge". However, it isn't just Frankenstein who desires this. Within the first few pages it is clear that Walton himself is fuelled by the same desire. When Frankenstein realises this he chastises his new friend: "Unhappy man! Do you share my madness? Have you drunk also of the intoxicating draught?" Indeed, much of the novel revolves around university and studying. However, none of those in this line of academic and scientific pursuit seem to feel any sense of contentment or happiness. No, true happiness in the novel seems only to be found in nature.

In direct contrast to those who seek 'knowledge' are those who are contented with the world around them. Frankenstein himself comes to the conclusion "how much happier that man is who believes his native town to be the world". The suggestion here is that happiness comes from connecting with nature. When his experiment has gone horribly wrong what does Victor do? He travels into the mountains to find peace " in the magnificence, the eternity of such scenes, to forget myself and my ephemeral, because human, sorrows". Time and time again, nature is seen to offer solace and happiness.

Shelley's use of language also projects a love of nature. Consider the natural metaphors used when Victor describes his childhood:

"I feel pleasure in dwelling on the recollections of childhood, before misfortune had tainted my mind, and changed its bright visions of extensive usefulness into gloomy and narrow reflections upon self . . . I find it arise, <u>like a mountain river</u>, from ignoble and almost forgotten sources; but <u>swelling as it proceeded</u>, it became <u>the torrent</u> which, in its course, has swept away all my hopes and joys".

In this early passage, Shelley is introducing a link between nature and human emotions. This link is found in many places throughout the novel.

Nature seems to have an almost mystical quality in this extended passage from Victor:

"I contemplated the lake: the waters were placid; all around was calm; and the snowy mountains, 'the <u>palaces</u> of nature,' were not changed. By degrees the <u>calm and heavenly</u> scene <u>restored</u> me, and I continued my journey towards Geneva.

The road ran by the side of the lake, which became narrower as I approached my native town. I discovered more distinctly the black sides of Jura, and the <u>bright</u> summit of Mont Blanc. I wept like a child. "<u>Dear</u> mountains! my own <u>beautiful</u> lake! how do you welcome your wanderer? Your summits are <u>clear</u>; the sky and lake are blue and placid. Is this to prognosticate <u>peace</u>, or to mock at my unhappiness?"

"The <u>immense</u> mountains and precipices that overhung me on every side, the sound of the river raging among the rocks, and the dashing of the waterfalls around spoke of a <u>power mighty as Omnipotence</u>"

"Ruined castles hanging on the precipices of piny mountains, the impetuous Arve, and cottages every here and there peeping forth from among the trees formed a scene of singular <u>beauty</u>. But it was augmented and rendered <u>sublime</u> by the mighty Alps".

It is clear from the positive vocabulary (underlined text) that Frankenstein is replenished by nature. However, it is not only Victor who feels this way.

Henry Clerval also acquires great pleasure from nature. When travelling with Frankenstein, Clerval "was alive to every new scene, joyful when he saw the beauties of the setting sun, and more happy when he beheld it rise and recommence a new day". Once again an intelligent and educated man is made almost surreally happy by nature.

Perhaps shockingly, even the creature derives much pleasure from nature: "My spirits were elevated by the enchanting appearance of nature". In much the same way as Frankenstein and Clerval, nature seems to lift the spirits of the creature.

Mary Shelley was not alone in using nature to restore characters; it was one of the major conventions of Romanticist literature.

Romanticism was a literary movement which began in the early 1800s. It had many facets, but one key convention is that Romanticist writers often used nature to explore emotions, Consider the William Wordsworth poem 'Tintern Abbey':

These beauteous forms,
Through a long absence, have not been to me
As is a landscape to a blind man's eye:
But oft, in lonely rooms, and 'mid the din
Of towns and cities, I have owed to them
In hours of weariness, sensations sweet,
Felt the blood, and felt along the heart;
And passing even into my purer mind,
With tranquil restoration:—feelings too
Of unremembered pleasure: such, perhaps,
As have no slight or trivial influence
On that best portion of a good man's life,
His little, nameless, unremembered, acts
Of kindness and of love.

In this poem, Wordsworth is reflecting on just how important natural landscape is. There are striking similarities with the words of Frankenstein, Clerval and the creature in the novel. But why is that?

Romanticists sought to learn from nature, to live in harmony with it. They fought against the Enlightenment scientists who attempted to control nature, feeling instead that there was much to learn from it. In a nutshell, Romanticists believed that nature could not be controlled. This is seen in the novel where the aggressive actions of Frankenstein lead to chaos and misery, but the enjoyment and study of nature leads to contentment. To summarise, Shelley presents a Romanticist view of science and nature in the novel.

So what is Shelley's point about happiness? It seems that she is saying there is much happiness and contentment to be taken from the world around us as we know it, and striving to know anything more than that which is already known will only lead to unhappiness.

Part 16

The Theme of Fate

One of Mary Shelley's major themes in 'Frankenstein' is the notion of fate. Those who believe in fate believe that the events of their lives are pre- determined and set – there is nothing that can be done to avoid them. As explained in another chapter, the structure of the novel enforces this theme. However, so does the plot.

Victor Frankenstein tells Walton "My fate is nearly fulfilled". He then further explains that "Nothing can alter my destiny; listen to my history, and you will perceive how irrevocably it is determined". Of course, by this time in the novel he is near death and not thinking rationally and it is therefore more interesting to rationally consider whether there is any evidence of fate in the life of Victor Frankenstein.

The first example relates to Frankenstein's childhood, where he explains that "curiosity, earnest research to learn the hidden laws of nature, gladness akin to rapture, as they were unfolded to me, are among the earliest sensations I can remember". Here it does indeed seem that Victor was 'fated' to become the scientist he ended up becoming. His earliest memories, i.e. a time in his life when he was not making deliberate choices but was acting out of instinct, had him researching the hidden laws of nature.

Similarly, when Frankenstein " thought of returning to my friends and my native town... an incident happened that protracted my stay". The incident in question here in chapter four is not clear, but whatever it was it could be seen as fate aiming to keep Frankenstein where he was.

Of course, it is easy to make a string of bad decisions and then blame then on fate, as indeed Frankenstein does: "destiny was too potent, and her immutable laws had decreed my utter and terrible destruction". It seems that fate can act as a scape-goat, but more than that it can be seen as integral part of the debate between nature and nurture. If fate is true, then 'nature' wins out over 'nurture'. What do I mean? Move onto the next chapter to find out!

Part 17

Nature vs. Nurture

The nature vs. nurture debate can be explained simply as this: are people the way they are because it is 'hard wired' into their brains from birth, or are they the way they are as a result of their personal experiences in life?

In the 1760s, Jean Jacques Rousseau's 'Emile' explored the nature of education and human beings. In this text, the writer argues that humans are born harmless, and that it is society which makes people either good or bad. Mary Shelley read this book, and explores its key questions in her novel.

The easiest way to look at this question is to consider the life of the creature, so that is where we shall begin. Obviously the creature has a horrible time and is treated badly by just about everyone he comes into contact with. After leaving Frankenstein he explains that "some attacked me". Clearly this treatment left its mark, as when he happens upon De Lacey, Felix and Agatha, he "longed to join them, but dared not. I remembered too well the treatment I had suffered the night before". This is evidence of nurture – the creature becomes hesitant and distant because of the way he is treated. He feels that "after my late dearly bought experience, I dared not enter".

One clear line of argument is that the creature was good, but the way it was treated by everyone made him turn into an evil murderer. This is certainly how the creature views himself, seen when he explains near the end of the novel that "my heart was fashioned to be susceptible of love and sympathy, and when wrenched by misery to vice and hatred, it did not endure the violence of the change without torture such as you cannot even imagine". The creature himself then feels that nurture has made him the evil monster he is, and that positive personal experiences would have, and still could, made him good.

Interestingly, the creature doesn't feel that his character is set. He tells Frankenstein "I was benevolent and good; misery made me a fiend. Make me happy, and I shall again be virtuous". The reader isn't sure whether the creature is bluffing or not, but we do know enough of his good deeds (such as chopping wood for the peasants) to suggest that there is good in this creature.

At this point there is a decision to make: was the creature 'born' good, but turned bad by the poor treatment he received? Or was he born evil? To help us decide, let's look at Frankenstein's description of the 'birth' in Chapter 5. This is a long passage but it is essential to study it in its entirety:

"I saw the dull yellow eye of the creature open; it breathed hard, and a convulsive motion agitated its limbs.

How can I describe my emotions at this catastrophe, or how delineate the wretch whom with such infinite pains and care I had endeavoured to form? His limbs were in proportion, and I had selected his features as beautiful. Beautiful! Great God! His yellow skin scarcely covered the work of muscles and arteries beneath; his hair was of a lustrous black, and flowing; his teeth of a pearly whiteness; but these luxuriances only formed a more horrid contrast with his watery eyes, that seemed almost of the same colour as the dun-white sockets in which they were set, his shrivelled complexion and straight black lips.

The different accidents of life are not so changeable as the feelings of human nature. I had worked hard for nearly two years, for the sole purpose of infusing life into an inanimate body. For this I had deprived myself of rest and health. I had desired it with an ardour that far exceeded moderation; but now that I had finished, the beauty of the dream vanished, and breathless horror and disgust filled my heart. Unable to endure the aspect of the being I had created, I rushed out of the room and continued a long time traversing my bed- chamber, unable to compose my mind to sleep. At length lassitude succeeded to the tumult I had before endured, and I threw myself on the bed in my clothes, endeavouring to seek a few moments of forgetfulness. But it was in vain; I slept, indeed, but I was disturbed by the wildest dreams. I thought I saw Elizabeth, in the bloom of health, walking in the streets of Ingolstadt. Delighted and surprised, I embraced her, but as I imprinted the first kiss on her lips, they became livid with the hue of death; her features appeared to change, and I thought that I held the corpse of my dead mother in my arms; a shroud enveloped her form, and I saw the grave-worms crawling in the folds of the flannel. I started from my sleep with horror; a cold dew covered my forehead, my teeth chattered, and every limb became convulsed; when, by the dim and yellow light of the moon, as it forced its way through the window shutters, I beheld the wretch—the miserable monster whom I had created. He held up the curtain of the bed; and his eyes, if eyes they may be called, were fixed on me. His jaws opened, and he muttered some inarticulate sounds, while a grin wrinkled his cheeks. He might have spoken, but I did not hear; one hand was stretched out, seemingly to detain me, but I escaped and rushed downstairs. I took refuge in the courtyard belonging to the house which I inhabited, where I remained during the rest of the night, walking up and down in the greatest agitation, listening attentively, catching and fearing each sound as if it were to announce the approach of the demoniacal corpse to which I had so miserably given life".

OK, let's begin by looking for evidence of 'nurture'. This is the birth of Frankenstein's creation, so how does he react? Not well! Look at the descriptive language here:

How can I describe my emotions at this <u>catastrophe</u>, or how delineate the <u>wretch</u> whom with such infinite pains and care I had endeavoured to form? His limbs were in proportion, and I had selected his features as beautiful. Beautiful! Great God! His yellow skin scarcely covered the work of muscles and arteries beneath; his hair was of a lustrous black, and flowing; his teeth of a pearly whiteness; but these luxuriances only formed a more <u>horrid</u> contrast with his watery eyes, that seemed almost of the same colour as the dun-white sockets in which they were set, his <u>shrivelled</u> complexion and straight black lips.

I have always found this passage fascinating. What did Frankenstein expect to happen? It seems he is totally shocked but why? He knew what lay before him and all it has done is begin to move. But it gets worse. Now let's look at how Frankenstein acts around his creation: '*I rushed out of the room*' and '*I escaped and rushed downstairs*'. The treatment of the creature here is terrible, and certainly backs up the idea that nurture makes us who we are.

Next, let's look for evidence in the same text that the creature was born good. Let's consider his actions in the passage:

"I saw the dull yellow eye of the creature open; it breathed hard, and a convulsive motion agitated its limbs".

So far so good – the creature has opened its eyes and begun to move around, just like a new born baby or a cute baby deer might do. These are the actions that caused Frankenstein to run away! Now look at this next passage carefully:

"He held up the curtain of the bed; and his eyes, if eyes they may be called, were fixed on me. His jaws opened, and he muttered some inarticulate sounds, while a grin wrinkled his cheeks. He might have spoken, but I did not hear; one hand was stretched out, seemingly to detain me, but I escaped and rushed downstairs".

Ignoring the deliberately negative language used here, let's consider just what it is the creature is doing:

1. He lifts up the bed curtain

2. He speaks

3. He smiles

4. He reaches out for Dr Frankenstein, his 'father'.

Are these not the actions of a child to a parent? The creature looks for his father, smiles when he finds him, tries to speak to him and reaches out, perhaps to cuddle him affectionately? The evidence is clear – the creature was not acting in any evil way here. The poor treatment that followed caused the creature to become more and more evil. It is certain that Mary Shelley is using the creature to argue for nurture over nature.

The application to real life is simple: Shelley is in agreement with Jean Jacques Rousseau: how we treat people will affect the person they become.

Part 18

Sample Question & Answer

"But it is true that I am a wretch. I have murdered the lovely and the helpless; I have strangled the innocent as they slept, and grasped to death his throat who never injured me or any other living thing. I have devoted my creator, the select specimen of all that is worthy of love and admiration among men, to misery; I have pursued him even to that irremediable ruin. There he lies, white and cold in death. You hate me; but your abhorrence cannot equal that with which I regard myself I look on the hands which executed the deed; think on the heart in which the imagination of it was conceived, and long for the moment when these hands will meet my eyes, when that imagination will haunt my thoughts no more.

"Fear not that I shall be the instrument of future mischief. My work is nearly complete. Neither yours nor any man's death is needed to consummate the series of my being, and accomplish that which must be done; but it requires my own. Do not think that I shall be slow to perform this sacrifice. I shall quit your vessel on the ice-raft which brought me thither, and shall seek the most northern extremity of the globe; I shall collect my funeral pile and consume to ashes this miserable frame, that its remains may afford no light to any curious and unhallowed wretch who would create such another as I have been. I shall die. I shall no longer feel the agonies which now consume me, or be the prey of feelings unsatisfied, yet unquenched. He is dead who called me into being; and when I shall be no more the very remembrance of us both will speedily vanish. I shall no longer see the sun or stars, or feel the winds play on my cheeks. Light, feeling, and sense will pass away; and in this condition must I find my happiness. Some years ago, when the images which this world affords first opened upon me, when I felt the cheering warmth of summer, and heard the rustling of the leaves and the warbling of the birds, and these were all to me, I should have wept to die; now it is my only consolation. Polluted by crimes, and tom by the bitterest remorse, where can I find rest but in death?

"Farewell! I leave you, and in you the last of human kind whom these eyes will ever behold. Farewell, Frankenstein! If thou wert yet alive, and yet cherished a desire of revenge against me, it would be better satiated in my life than in my destruction. But it was not so; thou didst seek my extinction that I might not cause greater wretchedness; and if yet, in some mode unknown to me, thou hast not ceased to think and feel, thou wouldst not desire against me a vengeance greater than that which I feel. Blasted as thou wert, my agony was still superior to thine; for the bitter sting of remorse will not cease to rankle in my wounds until death shall close them for ever.

"But soon," he cried, with sad and solemn enthusiasm, "I shall die, and what I now feel be no longer felt. Soon these burning miseries will be extinct. I shall ascend my funeral pile triumphantly, and exult in the agony of the torturing flames. The light of that conflagration will fade away; my ashes will be swept into the sea by the winds. My spirit will sleep in peace; or if it thinks, it will not surely think thus. Farewell."

He sprung from the cabin-window, as he said this, upon the ice-raft which lay close to the vessel. He was soon borne away by the waves and lost in darkness and distance.

'The reader sympathises more with the creature than with Frankenstein'.

Starting with this extract, explain how far you agree with this statement.
Write about:

How Shelley presents the creature and Frankenstein in this extract
How Shelley presents the creature and Frankenstein in the rest of the novel

[30 marks]

This extract comes from Chapter 24. The creature, finding Frankenstein to have died, explains his story to Robert Walton.

The following answer was actually submitted by a student (who wishes to remain anonymous) for use in this book. It is an incredibly impressive analysis.

Throughout the novel, Shelley's use of language, structure and form cause the sympathies of the reader to alternate between Victor and the creature. In this extract, Shelley creates pathos for the creature by humanising him through his love of nature and the lyrical language that he uses, and by making this passage the closing statement of the novel Shelley leaves the reader with a lasting impression of the creature's inherent good nature and sympathies for the creature rather than Victor.

In this extract, Shelley constantly associates the creature with nature. The creature describes himself as missing the 'sun and stars', the feeling of 'the winds play on [his] cheeks', and the 'cheering warmth of summer'. This imagery is overwhelmingly positive and the word 'play' connotes a childlike innocence and associates nature with the pure love and innocence a child feels before they are corrupted by the evils of the world. Through this, Shelley echoes ideas of Romanticism, in that all children are born good and are corrupted by the world, ideas that Rousseau wrote about in the famous Romantic text 'Emile'. By associating the creature with this childish innocence, Shelley directs the reader to be sympathetic towards him and to believe that the crimes that he committed were because of the corrupting nature of man, and were not his own fault. Shelley uses this throughout the novel, for example by giving the creature a diet of 'fruit and berries', which also brings him closer to nature and through this making the reader sympathise with him.

Another way that Shelley makes the reader sympathise with the creature is through his use of language. In this passage, the creature speaks with lyrical eloquence, such as the use of hypotaxis in the sentence starting with 'some years ago…', which creates a wistful and nostalgic tone and emphasises his love for nature, which creates sympathy for him as it emphasises his humanity. Shelley contrasts this with the harsh, guttural short sentences frequently used by Victor throughout the novel, such as 'fiend!' and 'wretch!'. By presenting the creature as the more eloquent and well-spoken of the two, the reader feels alienated from Victor's cruel language and therefore sympathising with the creature. Furthermore, Shelley's use of 'some years ago' reminds the reader of the tale that the creature told Victor in the mountains and makes the reader remember that this is not the first time that the reader has heard lyrical language from the creature. When he told his tale to Victor, the creature also uses poetic language and linguistic devices such as the simile 'like lichen on a rock'. Because of the Russian doll narrative form that Shelley employs, the voice of the creature is furthest away from the reader and filtered through both Victor's and Walton's biased view of the creature because of his appearance. This means that the reader never gets to hear the voice of the creature directly, but the fact that he still talks with such eloquence despite the biases of Victor and Walton means that the reader is further convinced of his inherent good nature and therefore sympathises with the creature.

Shelley also directs the readers' sympathies by using words from the lexical field of religion. The juxtaposition of negative religious words such as 'flames' and 'blasted', that are used to describe the creature's existence on earth and the living world with positive religious words such as 'ascend' and 'peace' that are used to describe dying highlights his unjust treatment and how 'miserable' his existence on earth has been, thus drawing pathos from the reader. Likewise, the anaphora of the phrase 'I shall' shows the creature accepting of his death and makes him into a martyr-like figure through his reference to a 'funeral pile' and 'torturing flames', which redeems him in the eyes of the reader. It is also presented as a contrast to Victor, who is described in the rest of the novel as not respecting the dead, dabbling in 'unhallowed arts' and 'playing' God, something that would have alienated particularly Shelley's original readers, making the sympathies of the reader lie more with the creature than Victor.

In conclusion, by ending with the creature telling his side of the story before his death, Shelley leaves the reader with sympathies for the creature rather than Victor. Throughout the novel, Shelley criticises Victor for experimenting with unnatural ideas and being the cause of his own demise through failing to be a proper parent towards the creature. In this final passage, Victor isn't mentioned at all suggesting that, despite the title, this is in fact the story of the creature rather than his creator, and therefore the closing impression of the reader is that of sympathy towards the creature.

Printed in Great Britain
by Amazon